MASTER MANDALAS
A MANDALA COLORING BOOK

ISBN-13: 978-1533249715
ISBN-10: 1533249717

FREE DOWNLOAD!

www.papeteriebleu.com/masterENG

YOUR DOWNLOAD CODE: MSTR8557

 @papeteriebleu

 Papeterie Bleu

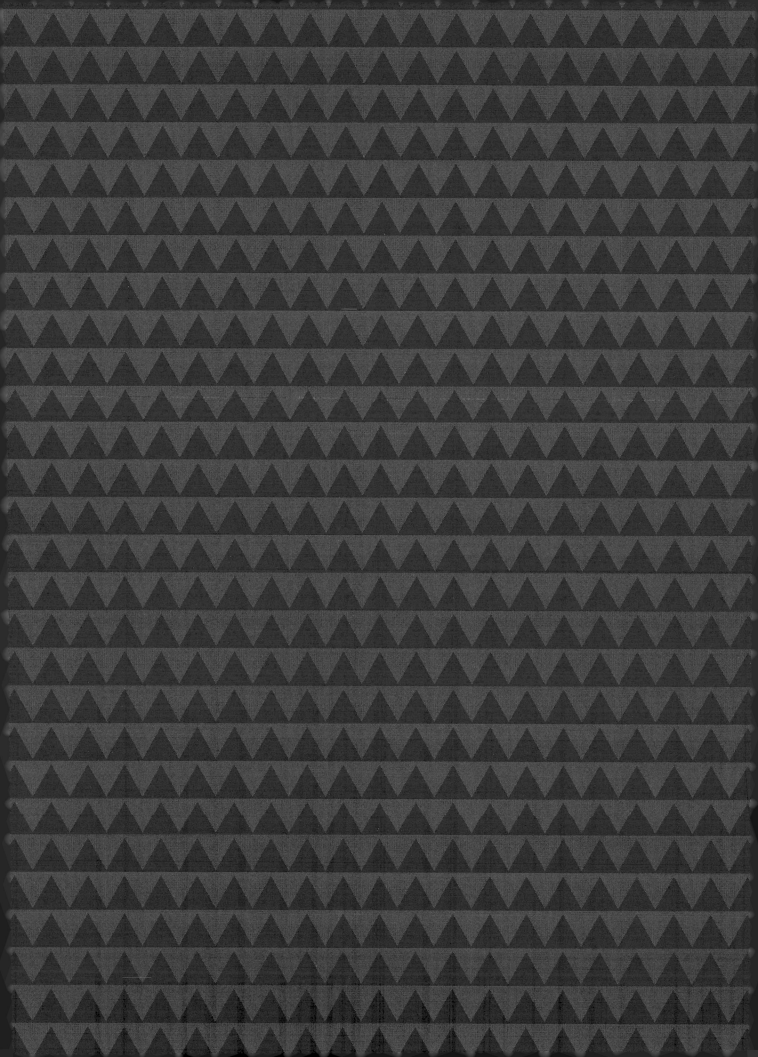

BE SURE TO FOLLOW US ON SOCIAL MEDIA FOR THE LATEST NEWS, SNEAK PEEKS, & GIVEAWAYS

[Instagram icon] @PapeterieBleu

[Facebook icon] Papeterie Bleu

[Twitter icon] @PapeterieBleu

ADD YOURSELF TO OUR MONTHLY NEWSLETTER FOR FREE DIGITAL DOWNLOADS AND DISCOUNT CODES

www.papeteriebleu.com/newsletter

CHECK OUT OUR OTHER BOOKS!

www.papeteriebleu.com

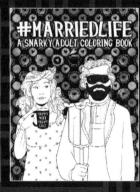

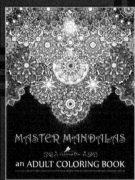

CHECK OUT OUR OTHER BOOKS!

www.papeteriebleu.com

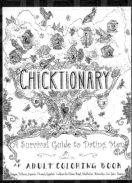

CHECK OUT OUR OTHER BOOKS!

www.papeteriebleu.com

 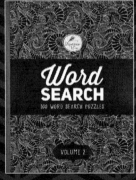   

Made in the USA
Middletown, DE
24 December 2017